THE GEORGIA POETRY PRIZE

The University of Georgia Press established the
Georgia Poetry Prize in 2016 in partnership with the
Georgia Institute of Technology, Georgia State University,
and the University of Georgia. The prize is supported by the
Bruce and Georgia McEver Fund for the Arts and Environment.

through a small ghost

through a small ghost

CHELSEA DINGMAN

The University of Georgia Press
Athens

Published by the University of Georgia Press
Athens, Georgia 30602
www.ugapress.org
© 2020 by Chelsea Dingman
All rights reserved
Designed by Rebecca A. Norton
Set in 11/15 Baskerville
Printed and bound by Sheridan Books, Inc.
The paper in this book meets the guidelines for
permanence and durability of the Committee on
Production Guidelines for Book Longevity of the
Council on Library Resources.

Most University of Georgia Press titles are
available from popular e-book vendors.

Printed in the United States of America
24 23 22 21 20 P 5 4 3 2 1

Library of Congress Cataloging-in-Publication Data
Names: Dingman, Chelsea, author.
Title: Through a small ghost / Chelsea Dingman.
Description: Athens : The University of Georgia Press, [2020] |
Series: The Georgia Poetry Prize
Identifiers: LCCN 2019026431 | ISBN 9780820356570 (paperback) |
ISBN 9780820356563 (ebook)
Classification: LCC PR9199.4.D565 A6 2020 | DDC 811/.6—dc23
LC record available at https://lccn.loc.gov/2019026431

for women and children, in every iteration—

you are as far as invention, and I am as far as memory.

—Susan Stewart

CONTENTS

ii.

ACKNOWLEDGMENTS

Thanks go to the following publications in which these poems first appeared:

Acre Books/Cincinnati Review: "Pathology"

Arcadia: "Traveling through Tennessee in January"

Baltimore Review: "Memento Mori"

Bennington Review: "Accident Report: After the Baby Dies at Birth"

Cherry Tree: "Matrimony as Indefensible Human Experiment"

Cincinnati Review: "Manner of Death"

The Collapsar: "Ephemera"

Colorado Review: "For Our Daughter"

Crab Orchard Review: "How a Woman Uses the Wind"

Day One; Amazon Book Review: "Letter from the Gulf Coast"

EcoTheo Review: "Uninhabitable Sphere" and "Thy Kingdom Come / Thy Will Be Done,"

Frontier Poetry: "(I Refuse to Pray)," "Torii Field," and "Instructions for Resurrection [of Our Marriage, if Nothing Else]"

Grist Journal: "Letter to My Future [Ex]"

Hypertrophic Literary Journal: "Postscript"

Indiana Review: "Redaction"

Iron Horse Literary Review: "The Wife as Scarecrow"

The Journal: "A World within a World"

Juxtaprose: "How to Survive"

LitMag: "Anniversary with Yellow Iris"

Los Angeles Review: "Wintersong"

Narrative Northeast: "Confession"

New South Journal: "As the Light Changes"

Ninth Letter: "Chimera"

Normal School: "How Briefly the Body"

Phoebe: "Persistent Complex Bereavement Disorder (Complicated Grief)"

Pittsburgh Poetry Review: "Song from a Drowning City (Legato)"

Pleiades: "Fugue" and "Unsigned Letter to My Stillborn Daughter Nine Years Later"

Prairie Schooner: "Intersections"

Quiddity: "When a Mother Is Not the Wind but the Window" and "Revisions"

Radar Poetry: "On Our Tenth Anniversary, My Husband & I Watch Tropical Storm Andrea Tear the Doors Off the Lanai," "Self-Portrait as God with a Stillborn Inside," "Conceptual Diagram Illustrating How Humans Are Structured and Formed," "Let the Night Come, Monstrous, & Make Use of Us," "We Didn't Read the Fine Print," and "Re-petition"

Sycamore Review: "Hunger [or the Last of the Daughter-Hymns]," winner of the Wabash Prize for Poetry (2017)

Tahoma Literary Review: "Hillsborough County Aubade"

Tinderbox: "If I Had Given Her Just One Bottle, She Would Still Be Alive"

TriQuarterly: "When the World"

Tupelo Quarterly: "The Werther Effect" and "Why I Stay"

Water~Stone Review: "Aftermath," winner of the Jane Kenyon Poetry Prize (2017)

I thankJay Hopler for encouraging me to write any experience I wanted to write and who showed me that brilliance can be fair and unfailing. I thank John Nieves for never failing to support me or push me and for being magical when I needed him to be. He knows what my manuscripts are doing before I do. I want to thank Traci Brimhall, who taught me to say what I mean and to find my voice again. I'm not sure I had ever given myself permission to take up space in this manner before working with her. Thank you to my students: you taught me far more than I taught you. I wrote this while I was wholly enthralled with all of the beauty you were putting into the world. Thank you to all of the poets, past and present, whose words are the constant music that bring me such joy. Thank you to the graduate students I was working with at this time, as well as to the entire English Department at the University of South Florida. I was so wonderfully supported by all of you, to whom I will always be grateful. Finally, thank you to the team at UGA Press for taking this leap with me again. I am beyond grateful for your kindness, your brilliance, and your faith in me.

Thank you to my family: Mom and Marcel, Laine and Shelby. To my sons, Hunter and Sawyer, who have made me someone else entirely. To my husband, Chris, who I've shared more years of my life with than we've been apart. And to those who can't be with us but are with us still & still & still: my love is unequalled.

through a small ghost

i.

MEMENTO MORI

I am what you will wear forever.

I walk carefully, so as not to jostle you inside me.

It is early. I came to this open field to have words

with the sky. A chapel of bones, my body is

the house you will forget how to breathe in.

I've already been warned, the doctors talking

about syndromes & chromosomes. *Remember*

everything will die. What reminder will you leave me

with? This sad architecture of bone & bristle

& sackcloth. This vanitas. On your walls,

I hired a woman to paint a forest. The ceiling, a night

sky. I wanted to give you the world. What mother has ever

been more holy? Rain is coming & coming

in the distance. *Let us refrain from sinning.* Tell me, again,

about the man who threw his daughter

from the Skyway Bridge, I want to ask. The body,

almost all water. *Does it hurt to drown?*

There is something exotic about housing an idea.

At the end of this longing, there will be almost

three hundred days I can't account for.

I mean: you are the absence of landscape.

I mean: in case of fire, I'd save you first.

UNINHABITABLE SPHERE

In the hours a child bends
into a labyrinth, who sees the hours
building in me this absence?
I asked for a city
to rebuke the river
I am. I asked for more sea
-sons. The country of my mother
that I gave up years ago. A woman
I wove from sand
& syllables. The phrases
thrown away when her body
failed us. I follow
the hollows in the orphaned
earth, but I refuse
the fence, the dam,
the log-laced river bottom.
The departed, like velvet
-cloaked bells. Each ovary,
a diamondful satchel.
Where are the minutes I will disappear in?
I thought a child would make me
immortal. But only the hours bear
a child. Slick. Indistinct.
Reeking of fertilizer & coffee grounds.
Sometimes, I want to go. The child will not grow
closer. I will not be distracted.
What fanfare is there in being
brave? I reach into the ground & feel
hundreds of years. Waiting mouths.

The hours that I won't be known.
A heaven that exists to empty
a mother of ghosts.
Of all of this possibility.

WHEN A MOTHER IS NOT THE WIND
BUT THE WINDOW

Copenhagen, Denmark

There is only the moon: the one face it shows
to the world. And there is never time for sleep.

Let us learn the sea, presiding over craggy rock. Let us
learn the tragedy of winter days that light won't touch.

On an island, the casual violence of rain is sometimes
the little that I can hold. Let me show you this landscape:

the rooms that are built to hold us; the city, like a question
so strange we care only for the windborn canals

uncalmed by boats; the buildings that flank us. The beauty
in not knowing where we are. Let us not miss each other

here. I have turned out to be more useless than I intended:
all ornament & sheen, little function. There are many things

I have seen that I can't speak of. But I have no memory.
Mirror & smudge & filter, I am what you'll make of me.

INTERSECTIONS

A mare lies alone in a field, her belly
distended, ribs like ladder rungs. Every few
minutes, her body quakes. The minstrel

wind shakes the oaks, as she spits
& shakes. I've seen this before:
the way a woman's body reaches

for its own ruin. Between the ilium,
the sacrum. A head driven into hard bone.
The alae's pearled wings that push back.

In the 18th century, the sacrum was believed
to be indestructible. The sacred bone.
But so much of birth is destruction—

the vertebrae, the bodies, the promontory.
Where & when & where. The intersection
of all parts. A cathedral's bronze doors

opening. The sudden obedience
of warring states. A labour that can be
outlasted. And, sometimes, a good birth

is merely a gasp of air. Blood. Shit.
The cathedral, its windows kicked out.

SELF-PORTRAIT AS GOD
WITH A STILLBORN INSIDE

Here is the room that made you a saint.

Here is the well. Your body, soon excavated
from mine. A little voice, not yours. Not divine—

here is the mother I might've been. The months

of preparation. The end of times. An era of false
imprisonment. My water will break & flood you

out. I'll wait for a sigh. The soft smack of your skull

on bloody thighs. This captivity is my fault. I want
to keep you longer. *Let there be light.* There is no bucket,

no rope. This isn't a nursery rhyme. *Let the earth bring forth*

living creatures after their kind. I have given warmth
& water to the earth. The plants & birds. The dry

seed of you trapped inside me. I have multiplied.

I have given everything to liken myself to the rime.
Beware of the body-lie. Body-quiet. The spirit

body. Believe me: childbirth is war. Let the blade

learn you. Let your throat soften against it.
Let the rules of war not apply. Here, creation

theory ends with thrashing. A drowning.

A body pulled from the dark & soldered
to the sky. This morning I made: keep it.

Only one of us is lying. I'll be just fine.

POSTSCRIPT

Tell me to lie down in the snow.
Tell me to track the deer, if only to run my fingers through their fur.

Tell me about regret—

      the sky always on its knees. The slight breeze
      brushing the backs of my hands
      not evidence of angels.

Tell me about death. How a daughter dies
inside her mother. How the clocks kneel.
How the sky is a thing to be worn.

A wind chime on my mother's porch.
The prairies. The constant wind
tears through me like a new language.
Like it's whispering *empty empty empty*

Daughter-haunt: forgive the ground,
calling & calling. You couldn't stay here.

Here: the crows circle.

Here: there's blood in the drain,
clogged with hair.

Late fall: my eyes, tongued open. Hands,
hopeful for the miracle
of a hot shower.

A new war on the news.

Windows open at dusk, the musky air is juſt
-ice.

       I hear a small nightsong in the hush
       of snow. I don't know if resurrection
       is real.
               The birds, gone

       south. My breaths disappear
       into the night where my daughter is

       a diſtant ſtranger. This diſtance I have
                  no name for.

ACCIDENT REPORT:
AFTER THE BABY DIES AT BIRTH

First, I asked for
mercy, when mercy
was a small sliver
of light. My bones
softened by the body
leaving them. You asked
questions, green
tea in hand. Some
lemon. A cleanse
of sorts, as I refused
your prayers. The sky,
faithless, darkening
again. You wanted
to know what's next,
when we would try
again, what every doctor
had to say. I was
an empty stall
in a gas station
bathroom. I said, never.
But now I say
now, let's try now,
before I lose
my nerve. But you
don't want to touch me
yet. You eye my body
like a broken trough
looking for any sign
of seepage. I drink

from the mug. You move
away, the way the wounded
animal moves before
it tucks tail & runs. Every
good-bye is unnecessary
after holding something
as it dies. I want to feel full
again, I say. The door, open
as a mouth. You raise
your hand over my body
& ask, where does it
hurt? But I can't say
everywhere. I can't
say, it hurts everywhere
I'm touched. I can't
say, touch me every
-where. Please.

HOW A WOMAN USES THE WIND

Bones & ash collect in the weeds
& I want to tell my mother

how it is to live without sleep. How
I dream while awake. These two parts

of myself, inseparable. How I want her
to be alive to see the things I will

survive. But she's somewhere
hefting her own ashes. The names

of gods I've disobeyed. My daughter,
with her, as thin as our breaths

in winter. I learn to hold onto heaven
& feel rain fall against my cheeks.

I swear to do everything right. But
no matter who I lie to, no one listens.

The wind swirls around my body,
wanting as I want. To remake

our bodies from ashes. Wanting
to be healed by turning away.

CONFESSION

Like you, I am built out of sky:
light & air I use to mend
the bones I owned before your body roamed
free & I made of myself this silence
large enough to multiply
in my womb where our daughter
died when I was afraid to be touched
by water or anything else. She was pretty,
wasn't she? Our daughter, not your excuse
for vanishing. Her ribs, like folded wings.
I should've known faith is like a father.
Here. Not here. You are like the god
I called when the cramps came. You raise
the forests where sacrifices are the trees.
Not a baby. Not human need. I, myself, am
alien now. Something not quite realized.
A sentence missing its verbs. The blue
-bellied birds are back at the door, the sky
burned from their feathers. In the fields
of my body, a pond. So I may know
how to be full when consequence is a sea
-son. The sky refusing rain. The months
we've pretended to know ourselves.
But what is grief? A noun we can't hold
with our hands? A hallelujah? o ghost,
o mother-grave——, hallelujah.

INSTRUCTIONS FOR RESURRECTION
[OF OUR MARRIAGE, IF NOTHING ELSE]

Don't tell me about the dead
leaves littering the gutters, your fists
& jaw clenched at the impossibility
of order. Don't tell me a name
can be buried in the skin
when the sky is suffering
again. Don't tell me about our child—
how heaven is a holding cell
for the incorruptible. How she'll always be
young. Don't tell me about
impossible love. I invoked your god,
but it isn't love he's interested in
selling. Don't tell me you're sorry
as you try to touch me. Don't touch me
like I'm wind, instead of the trash
bag bullied by wind in the gas station
parking lot. Tell me, instead, you hold
my emptiness like a window
holds the sky. Tell me god
-less clocks will kneel for us.
Tell me rain is the sky's apology.
Tell me forgiveness belongs to the trees
trundled into split-rail fences. Tell me
talk of trees is the real crime
when I can't talk of the missing
child. That blame is the sparrow
that thrusts itself against my ribs
until it crushes its own skull.

LETTER TO MY FUTURE [EX]

                    Where time is a country
we can't revisit, I save the closed

rooms of my body: root & stem, rock
            & riverbed. If there is anything near

-holy, a woman's body is. Sanctuary.
                    Sanitarium. You say you prayed for me

while our daughter was dying
            in one room or another that I have yet

to name. I need you to sober & sink
            your teeth into early morning, still

dark at six am. We need to memorize
            the dead—; or do they memorize us?

Have you ever been inside a sanctuary
                    so lacking? Sometimes, I am

delirious with daughters. The thrum of names
            I've been given, locked in the dumb hollow

of dead throats. *What we grow inside ourselves*
            isn't safe. Safe & less safe, I lie

next to you. I love & tussle & disappoint.
                    The country of night spills

over us. We won't be persuaded
        that what was once living is still

living. Our penance is believing
                in the abstract dark. In the heart

as flesh, as trope. In every creature & closed
        room that will cease to exist.

EPHEMERA

Before our future

         appeared, pink

& pouty lipped, you ran fingers

over

         taut skin on my stomach

& felt her move within me

               like water. Maybe it was a last kick

or backflip

you felt. I wished, then, as sun

         invaded the blinds,

             that we were

childless. Just for a second. Just

                 long enough to feel

guilty. The world outside the windows

         making me wish for

quiet. Maybe a wish isn't enough

to stop a mouth,

like gills, from taking

in water. But

her still face, cold & closed

as we kissed it,

taught me love

is not a fence

to tether our bodies to. That,

of all the dead

I'll sorrow, no one else

will make me so

terrible. So terribly

alive.

HUNGER
[OR THE LAST OF THE DAUGHTER-HYMNS]

i.   (n) *a feeling of discomfort or weakness caused by lack of food,*
coupled with the desire to eat—

> as I talk to wind winnowing my ribs into wind
>   chimes. I swallow small coins from the counters,
> wanting change my body can keep. I ſtand

>   on the ſtreet corner in the rain & coax water
> into my mouth like a woman who doesn't know
>   the fullness of the sea. My mother worked

> three jobs to feed our family. Now, I horde
>   toilet paper & paper towels in spare closets
> with cans of soup & creamed corn. The wind

>   hollows the oaks. Their bones don't know
> what it is to break, but I am a hollow
>   inſtrument, a sacred text. Daughter[less].

ii.   (v) *have a strong desire or craving for*

> a body inside my body—
> a child, a man.

> Fields, full. The sun,
> aflame. Fear like a shot

-gun, an aborted flight
plan, people jumping

from buildings. But
my daughter, I draw back

down. The one I lost.
The ones I have left

to lose. Like snow—
the bodies that are ours

for a season. For less.

iii.   (v) *to feel or suffer through lack of food*

                    the weak sunrise

in my daughter's new

                         silence. My skin, a loose

sheet. Her clavicle, hip

                         -bone, head. My cervix,

thinned. Her body, an offering. A prayer

        I whisper as I tear

                         new maps in a lucid dream

where I live alone

    & she folds herself into a crane

        to hang from the ceiling

of someone else's womb.

WINTERSONG

December's cold comes to pity us again,
fields stormed by dry riverbeds & dead leaves.
I'm afraid, but I don't want to tell you.
The baby hasn't moved & there is blood
where there shouldn't be. My body,
less godlike when still, cleaves to yours, almost

whole when someone else is inside. Almost
sane, I imagine our daughter again,
the vine-like cord wrapped around her body.
On the news, there is a woman who leaves
her child on a schoolroom floor, covered in blood,
& no one is safe. Not even us. You

know the truth: I've only ever loved you.
Even when we were power lines, almost
breaking under snow. There's blood
on my thighs & I call you home again,
but we've never been people to choose who leaves.
Tonight, each psalm we know is a body

broken off in our teeth, the baptism of a body
we will never touch back from blue, but you
sing anyway, hands clasped like leaves
around my swollen belly. Something is always almost
breaking inside me when you touch me. Again,
birth is sometimes about destruction: blood

& shit & sound. Or no sound. Just blood
we want to reinvent inside the body—
what happens if we break all the way open again?
Without the tiny bloom of her, will I be enough for you?
In this failure: hunger-songs like a firing squad. Almost
brave, I want to run for our lives, to leave

this cold ground beneath us, the leaves
like ghosts I can't give away. Like blood.
We were almost in love yesterday. Almost
sane. I turned you on, my body
swollen like sky you want to part. A promise you
will love me when you can't. Again,

we blossom & break, leaves in a gutter. Again,
blood when I bend. For a few months, you
were almost real. The lyric, longing a body.

THE WERTHER EFFECT

Do you think the saying is true:
when someone dies, a library burns down?
—*Allison Benis White*

Maybe *mother* is the verb.

To have a child is to learn we are all dying
by degrees. I want to bring my child

home. To wrap her body in bedsheets
& hold my hand over her mouth

like an open flame. Is there a heaven with less

razor wire & blood? In the next county,
a woman slips while cutting down a razor wire

fence on her property. With each
small movement, she tears herself apart.

I want to hurt like that.

Why must our sentences burn?
A sentence, now, the slag of fog

over the fields.
The safety of a secondhand.

WE DIDN'T READ THE FINE PRINT

But, of course, the poppy fields died.
We were always praying to straw grasses.
Lime trees. A river in slow motion.
Sound takes years to get here, so

these words will reach the future
mother I might be. Death is like a perfect
strand of pearls pulled from a throat.
Like a child, shiny & blue. This, after

years of condoms, the Pill, a wedding.
An IUD they guaranteed me was safe.
But what guarantee of safety is there
in anything, let alone the life span

of a cluster of cells? Now they're asking:
Are you okay? Are you okay? Are you—?
[insert pain here] The white mountain
grows in the window, a consequence

of winter & time. It's impossible to say
how long the poppies grew wild around us,
but I remember them here. Their crimson
bodies, brilliant & brimming with sun.

REVISIONS

sometimes you don't die
but bloom back like the soil long dead
under snow & you are born to this stain of sun
creeping under the blinds of the body I inherited
from the ghosts of mothers, inhabited
by ghosts of long grasses & stem
cells & storm drains, a body made by wind
that gathers in the fields, the beheaded
dandelions that I drink from, the stars
always revising themselves

                                  & sometimes
neither one of us dies, but we draw
a country in the wet sand beside a pier
& the water is calm & warm
as we show the sky our teeth & I am your mother
& my mother isn't the woman I don't want
to be, & a song isn't an anthem or a dirge
but your body as it fills me full
& I am not a casket, the dead
like fillings in my teeth & we practice living
longer with expensive creams & vitamins,
with broccoli & early bedtimes & boot camp
workouts &

                      I would do all of this
so you'd hold my name under your tongue
like a pill I've been given to help me sleep in another universe
where you're not on the porch, your hair back
-lit by morning, cushioned by the sun,
& when I wake, I try to imagine you
there, alive, & I want to live forever

before I remember there is no forever
when you have already died so
many times, the light spilling over
my splayed body, your small body
delivered blue
                    & sometimes
we are the dead, the blue, the ghosts
of trees & rivers, the countries
where there is no one to damn
us & someone else tends the light
                              & sometimes
there is only me, this light untended,
this world I don't want to wake in.

FUGUE

There is a river, & in its mouth, the holocaust
night I gave birth to a broken mirror,

the shard that stuck in a man's neck.
He pulled it out & that was the beginning

of blood. The nightmares. Being chased
through a small ghost

town, windows shut & boarded, only shadows
to command: *break or break me.*

I had a god, once. Somewhere, I think
I'll know how to be full & limber

& not the husk that held the crowning
dark. Not the woman, unbelieved.

He hit me. The night the baby died,
I was tired of the blank stars dying quietly

years from here. I should've braced myself—
his fists like arrowheads. The glass

river, leaking bodies. *I'll fucking kill you.*
Even now, I close my eyes & hear water.

There is no baby. There never was.

AFTERMATH

The fields say *future* when they mean *failure*
after the Florida sun is done

with them. The way *failure* is a womb,
empty & frayed. What is a woman

is a wife is a mother? The soft cull
of the wind hollowing my mouth?

The salt-wounded water. Dead
squirrels & cockroaches that swell

the sewers. What can I ask for
other than a child to love

the country of my body, each
tattered lawn & Queen palm?

Is salvation the days I'm lucky enough to know
sun? Or are my failures

smaller than a season? Miscarriage
is an interesting word for what a woman

can't hold. A child. A presidency.
Clemency, when all faith is gone. I used

to pray for a daughter. Now, cruelty
is forgiveness. Field. Body. Country.

REDACTION

I lose the baby   quietly   disappearing

       from mirrors   like the body at the bottom of a lake

unmaimed   I have loneliness I can't name

ghosts I can't give away   wind that threads the hydrangeas

a pond where water used to pray   I'm tired of trying

       to be sane   my husband wants sex   to bind us

        each tenderness   so rude   the sky

faithless   the world in orbit   the grasses greening beneath us

       without bidding   I bid the rain to come

I search for answers in bathwater that won't part   in rain

that won't fall   my body   made of water   I don't want

       next door   a girl plays in gutters

       swamped by brown pollen

no water to wash anything away   she points at the storm drain

       at something lost that she can't name

every temporary emptiness   borrowed from the sky

       a world made   *& unmade*

HISTORIOGRAPHY

Orphan is the child
   whose parents are water.

  The sun strikes the lilies,
     unforgiving as splintered glass

& my body learns to run.
   Listen: nightwind. Belly laughs.

     The cicadas' wild cacophony.
       Water-haunt, I am only ever

visiting. All of this living
  & I want the attention of water.

    I try to be so transparent.
    The window, the windshield—:

how many creatures will beat themselves
     against my breasts?

    I learn to want. To hold others
   when I can't be held.

I learn home is no-land
  & every-land. Horror

    is drought. A field of flies
     & dead sparrows. The child

  singing to the dark
    that won't stay.

CHIMERA

A new baby I bury
inside myself with peppermint
leaf & red raspberry leaf
& chasteberry—fertility teas
I purchase online. Each month,
pissing on white strips
like tarot cards, foretelling
the future: ovulation, pregnancy, mis-
carriage. I could be magic.
Perhaps. Perhaps,
it's sleight of hand & I am
the magician, hell-bent
on pulling a child
from the burned
-out rubble
in my belly. Ground
zero now, I erect
a new body from tails
& tongues & fur. From fumes
clinging to the skies
of my womb. Perhaps,
I am a good liar.
Perhaps, I don't exist
at all, my body
a myth I've told
for so long, I forget
I breathe fire. That every part
of me was made
for killing.

TO THE SPONTANEOUSLY ABORTED FETUS

Did you wish to live

cocooned by my lungs? Before you were

the creature who ate her own

hair in the womb? Before the hair

didn't reappear. Appear to me.

Just this once. Pretend you're old enough

to speak. Who but the living can speak

for the dead? I borrowed a hurricane

from the sky

to tell me how some storms rail

& others rally. *I want you to hurt me*

I said to the sky & I woke

with a belly full of wet stones. But the sun

doesn't hurt today. Today, marigolds

gold the garden. The oaks

sway. Gone, the stitch of air

I ate for dinner months ago. The heart

-burn I can't explain.

HOW BRIEFLY THE BODY

How briefly the body is a story
        where everything matters,

even its name. The oaks outside
        dip & dangle in the wind. Sun

dapples deep-green leaves, ripe
        with spring rain. But in the body, I am

a transient. I've had a host of women's names
        kneel down inside me. When I can't

name the reasons I listen to rain
        fill me like words on a page, the body

is a story of devotion: it knows the cost of moving
        into morning, asking to be spared

nothing. I asked only to be alive,
        but I can't know where I'll find climax,

or if denouement looks like my mother
        kneeling, as she asks for bare skin

to enter like the first bars
        of a hymn. In the body, all things

have an end. I can't yet know how it is
        to enter morning & be left

with myself—every story I've known
　　carried off like tree pollen

in the white spring wind. But I enter, however
　　briefly. Asking nothing.

WHY I STAY

Among couples who had a stillbirth, nearly 60 percent
broke up within ten years, while close to half of couples
who had a miscarriage broke up within a decade
—Amy Norton, Reuter's Health, 2010

Because you are the prayer,
today. Because you are the train
's sutures cutting through land. Because
you untangle land & houses
& silences I hold in my ribs
like the ghosts of children
in ghettos.

Because I am a stitch of lake
-effect snow on the Gulf.

Because you are here, today. The map
of your body, late fall,
under the canopy of a palm
tree. Because, today, your face
is troubled in sleep. Because
you've been dreaming you are
the poppy field I bury myself

inside, the earth, the other
side of the river
where the women I've been
stand like accusations.

Because you dream them now, so I don't
have to—

the woman who didn't sew
clothes onto her child's back or follow her
like sky. The woman who birthed
a still child, yet can't forget
how her body once moved.

Because of you, today, this address.
The addresses I've entered for the last time.

Because I am still here.
Because I've become this country

that I can't keep. Because
you've remade the map
into a map, remembered.

Remember?

I am the night
itself. Even the dark
can be forgiven.

ON ACCIDENTS & THE COLD NIGHT

for my grandmother

Did the child lay herself down in the road before
                                        the truck passed?

The driver, drunk.
Her mouth, empty as moon.

In the dark, the cold, the night that she fell to
avoid, I turned / I turned /
I turned from her for the man I had to feed first, for the field
                        that begged water to blur

            the yellow edges of want. What have I to brave
                        if not the daughter that lays herself down

            before I'm ready? *Hold your breath
through the tunnels,* I used to say on our way home

            in the car. On the bridge & over the train
tracks: *raise your feet for luck.*   But no!

                The wind trembles the weeds, the lake
                                half-dead from cold.

She was dead in the road for hours before anyone noticed.
                                Her body, adored
by lamplight. Lying there. There: the night
pressed to her flesh like I would have at bedtime,
                        in her room. The weight of her

against me. Against forgetting: this thin wind
        that travels through me, that turns me from mother
            of three to mother of two, to mother

                            of the dead, the road, the roadkill
left by a man's tires. My body, this longing large
                            enough to hold a child,
now stationless

            & built on breath. I told her to stay
inside / before

            I left. To stay out of the road. That I had to work
to breathe / to clothe / to clamor / to soldier

& mother & meander & I can't be done
with love. Nor the terrible lake beyond the turn
                        in the road. She could've drowned.

With my sight & longing. The day, laying itself down
                        in the ground. At a distance, the driver saw

a small folded package. A paper crane. Perfect
        & utilitarian. Later: frozen to the ground, her fists stiff,

the road lays open as a wound. It stays. Like the loons
by the lake in winter. They do not wander or wonder
            about us. They sing. They sing of nostalgia

                        & the fraught sky. The fragile child
                            -hoods we give away
without realizing how
        significant the hours. There: my mother taught me
            to mother is to kneel is to bow is to offer oneself

to the sky. The winterflowers. The lake, lashed
                    to this landscape. And the answer is yes:

I loved beyond love. Beyond the wound
she cut herself from. Beyond the woods & graves & water. This
          fear that comes true as the sky kneels in the posture

of prayer. As the morning kneels before other children,
          rising from sleep in another room. The road, empty
except for a skiff of new snow.

I should be afraid. I should get up to greet them & smell their night
                                                  -sweat, fragile

sleep they have yet to sweep away. Through the window,
                    light threatens to break like bodies

          we claim when it's too late. Darling girl: *it's too late.*

The dead will daughter not at all.
How unwaveringly we're mistaken.

MICROCHIMERISM

Of debris—the dead can't be
reborn, but in my brain, ten years

of passenger cells. They circulate
in my blood as a reminder:

a mother is not a cure. The marrow.
The window that lets light

out. One child didn't live. Two
grow taller with the orchestra

hours. Lightwings of the street
lamps. The living folded into paper

lanterns in the garden. I gather
loss like ruined riverwater.

A ragweed stench. She smelled
as she will always smell. Her heart,

wet. A small plum I palmed.
What shapes does love take?

I am a host. Not Gaia. Nor god
-ess. Nor wound. Nor depression

glass. Nor the mouth saying *stay*
& *stay* & *stay*. I should say *the shovel*

struck dirt instead. I should say
the fields are burning. It's a small comfort

that I am the burial wrapping.
The dead are heavier in death.

I should be grateful. I should be
so many things I'm not.

(I REFUSE TO PRAY)

That's a lie. But Jesus, I don't know
you or your father.
My father & daughter are dead

& I am not equal to this
anger. I am the south Florida summer
rains that know no mercy. I am the knife

-edge of night. The edge of the pond
where someone once drowned.
Where have you been hiding?

Green blades of grass are ghosts
now. It's winter. Forty degrees.
Frost has set in. The alligators

have disappeared from water holes.
Only the crows sit on tile roofs, waiting
for what we'll throw away.

Charm me. Harm me. It's all the same.
In the distance: a pink sky. Sirens.
A stoplight, changing on a timer.

See my stomach? Look: it sags
like a six-month-old balloon. The skin
stretched into a makeshift shrine.

Can you hear me? I want
less sky. Less sun. Less
weather. Listen: the wind

is blessing every door.
In the hush of night
-fall, I almost hear snow,

even here. I am almost
home, in this body. Almost
something holy.

FOR OUR DAUGHTER

We spend the afternoon
watching wind stir Spanish moss
on a live oak's low branches,

as their twined shadows spin
on the sidewalks below.
The last time we saw her
was in Copenhagen. It was Christ

-mas, the last time you slung your hand inside
my shirt, over the bells of my ribs.
As the wind stirs my hair, you move

closer to me. I am skittish, the colt
newly walking on shaky stilts.
The gentle blue of her
still shows in your bones.

This is not love. It is what has become
of love. This is what an altar
looks like, our church rent

from the ground during a hurricane.
Who do you pray to now? I ask,
my hand over your mouth. The wind
uproots the tulips, yellow flames

flaming the yard. I imagine
their petals are bells we can't ring
at her gravesite, an ocean

between us, as you feather my throat
with your fingers. For a moment,
I forget & I'm surprised.
The wind collects old prayers

with tulip-limbs & white
wisps of moss, an offering
for another place, another hour.

HOW TO SURVIVE

Once: in the snow,
the streets empty of snowplows,
the birds gone
south, you thought you were
alone. But you are
never alone. Earwigs scurry
out of the sink
drains. The mail arrives
each afternoon.
The sun comes
& goes. Fear the world
without snow.
How you will bear living
somewhere you don't know
yourself.

Tell yourself pain is normal.
A cliché.   The sky
at your feet. You feel pity
for the way it lies there. It has
no mother. No father. Yet,
you have the urge to stomp on it.
To beat it to death.

When the baby dies [because it will
die], blame yourself. Blame
your ugly, twisted bones. Blame
the veins that didn't feed her well
enough. Blame your legs for moving
too often. How could you forget?

                                     Forget
        the body. Forget the sound
        she made leaving you. The folds
        in her skin. You are a magician,
        but every trick has its flaws. You are
        too young to make room for this
        grief. It's summer again. You are
        feral in this heat.

Admit starving. You are
all ribs. A mother.
Not a mother. Some
-where in between. You sleep
& sleep, the dark
an old house
-coat that makes an absence
of your body. Define
yourself, nude
except for nude silk
panties. Is this
what you always hoped
you'd be?

You feel your dead
mother rise in you.
You recognize her
by her grief. By her fear.
By the river of her body, dark
with what others deposited
there. Ask to be forgiven.
Ask for distraction—
a startle of wind, shrill
at the windowpanes.

TORII FIELD

Trinity, Florida

You stand in a vanished airfield.
The wind, wild. Your daughter who is dead now
traffics the sound of old jet engines

to teach you how to sing. The sun tattering
your lips, you open your mouth wide & exhale

exhaust. You cradle the hurt
of her until you are a mother
again. You are alive. You praise

the daughter in you who is still hiding
in the dark crawlspace of your childhood

closet. You want to tell her everything
will be okay. That she is the house
& the house on fire. As the earth rotates

for no other reason. As you are missing
on every map. You want someone

to say *wake up*. That when you get home,
the nursery will be thick with the sweat
of a sleeping infant, the crackle of a monitor.

That shelter has always been the body.
Your made body. Hers. You can love

what hurts you until hurt is an airfield,
long a ghost. Until a song is as impossible as love.
But even if there were someone to make you

leave here, walk back the long miles
to that house, to the fires, to the flame

that adores you, would you know how
to be someone other than a mother
now? To be still & still breathing?

PERSISTENT COMPLEX BEREAVEMENT DISORDER (COMPLICATED GRIEF)

The truth is, that every death is violent.
—*Samuel Johnson*

Then let me know the violence of the last
day of sun. The violence of a thousand

orphaned forget-me-nots floating
in the fields. The women bent in child-

birth. The child who hanged herself
inside me before birth. Let me know

the violence that will be mine. I'm tired
of mourning what is lost here—the leaves,

rainfall collecting in the gutters, the doe
that used to visit my yard, midafternoon,

as my growing belly marked time.
It is months later & the doe is spared

the violence done in this body. I am
spared pleasure. Outside, the trees' limbs beat

their bodies in wind that has stitched itself
in a thousand strands of hair. The green season

recedes. Blackbirds circle above, beating
their bodies with threadbare wings. Beating

each other back from a dead creature
left in the street, as if one violence does

not beget another. But isn't that what
I'm supposed to want: violence that begins

with necessity? Some measure of mercy?

IF I HAD GIVEN HER JUST ONE BOTTLE, SHE WOULD STILL BE ALIVE

who mothers the mothers who tend the hallways of mothers
—Catherine Barnett

The breasts are a temporary food source.
I am a starved city.

I held my daughter, grey, curled into a comma.
Her hair caught fire in the hospital lights.

Someone said this isn't normal. Babies don't scream this much.
Someone said breastfeeding is best.
Someone broke.
Someone explained dehydration. A heart attack. Asystole.
I said amen. Amen. Amen.

And still, the doors open.
And still, the night comes.
And still, the terror of headlights stream past the passenger
side of the car.
And still, the babies in other cars.

Men are broken by less.

I offer her cremated body to the lake.
I offer the night our gods.
I offer myself to mothers. Others. The mouth.
The eye. The nipple.
To the dark gathering like children in the corners
of the room.
To the children in the corners of the room still
breathing.

I remember——, those who die a little
at my breast everyday. Those who survive
like a city on fire.

RE-PETITION

And think of the dream:
       the one where your father forgets his keys

            & lives, or the baby breathes
                 outside your body, or the toddler doesn't

                       fall from the ſtone basin
                       where you bathe

          him. And think of the skull
       as intact. The pupils,

                    unburſt. That silence
             where you lay down

your wanting
       as fire in a foreſt. And think

          of wanting as a shadow
               that attaches itself

                to the body without discretion
        or violence: the cattle's cries

amid harveſted crops,
       the child's cries—for a breaſt,

          for milk, for breath—
              the gentle blow

                                        of his first dead
                        goldfish, the empty bowl,

drought that lays itself down
        in the fields, one lit cigarette

                        from a car window
                                as the houses burn

                                as we rise & rise & the ground
                        browns, as we water & weed

and think of the wilderness—how long it has
                                suffered weather,

                the terrible trouble of sleep. And think
                        of *human* as *temporary:*

our brilliance for forgetting,
                like being burned

                        by the sun, again & again,
                                for the first time.

A WORLD WITHIN A WORLD

You say *mother* means [   ]. Maybe it means

genius. A plaything for the dark

world. The pretty one. The pear

tree. The axle grease. The weeping

willow alongside the winding

ſtreet. The jayhawk. Or, maybe it means

one of a thousand ſtrands of

hair

touched by the wind. Without feathers

or filthy nails or feces. Without voices

saying o [foolish] woman, o [lantern]

heart, o [loſt one]: remember

the children. Remember

when you were [

].

LET THE NIGHT COME, MONSTROUS, & MAKE USE OF US

> *people often name an object after the manner*
> *in which we destroy it*
> —Ben Lerner

Am I the red-eye? The receptacle.
The body where others leave themselves. Gutted,

you leave me to the rain.
You pretend a body can't be named—

the daughter we lost.

The woman you fucked to fuck
yourself sane.

What's in a name? I don't know

why we name a daughter who died in utero.
Why we don't call her grief.

Fuckery. Thief. I want to name what you did.

I want to name the blood. The hurt
of her. The shadow-prayer of her.

I want to name the dark.
I want to name you *bastard.*

I want.

I want my body to protest
yours. Hers. The bodies that died

inside me. Not once.

I want not to want
you. Even now. Even when.

LITANY [IN WHICH I GIVE MYSELF AWAY]

Everyday after I give birth, my body is less strange.
    Everyday, we grow estranged anyway. Like wainscoting
over the walls, you want a woman who forgets
    she is a woman. Have you forgotten? I want

the rain you salvaged from the retention pond
    in the backyard, golf balls & flywings & feathers
skimming the surface. Some water isn't meant
    for swimming, but you want to take our clothes off

& pretend swimming is the answer to my sagging
    belly, your wandering hands. The baby we buried
with the compost & coupons for formula in another
    country. Do you remember the rain in Copenhagen?

    Some violences we couldn't live with. The streets
teeming with tenement buildings & cemeteries.
We'd finally found a place where the dead outnumbered
    the living. A warscape older than we felt. I let you touch me

new in the bathroom of our one-room apartment,
    your hips ground into mine. Amid piss tests & pink lines
on sticks. Then, we were stateside again. Pregnant
    again. You stayed out until dawn every night. You stayed

until someone threw you out. You stayed anywhere
    new. You've always wanted to live in a movie,
but we weren't creative enough to keep a child
    alive, our sex life alive, the tulips trimming the yard

alive. It's rainy season again. The mulch molds
        the base of the live oaks that line our road, & the ſtory
where you cheated while I held our second child
        to my cheſt, while I cried & spit & ſtoried my way

                out of every night, while you flew to new cities
so you could forget us, our bed, the sour smell
        of spit-up & sweat, the wind barreling againſt glass
                doors, makes me a good pretender. Maybe

I should've known you cared more
        about being seen than seeing. Maybe
that makes me naïve or ſtupid or sorry. Later,
        I thought you were a prophet when you pushed me

                up againſt the night & ſtripped me so slowly
I thought I might like being sorry. Everyday
        now, we wake to houses like prayer flags, candy
                -coloured, their spines ſtitched into the sky.

Everyday, you touch me & I forget another
        name. The gutrot. The jealousy. The child
I won't mother. The woman you might've asked
        is this okay? as you turned yourself to water

                inside her. You say *love* like twenty-five years
                        of trembling is why we ſtay. Say *love*. Say it
        again. Say you're waiting for wind to break
                the glass. Say you thought about leaving.

Say I loved you all the wrong ways. I don't care.
        I want to live anyway. Say the mouth is meant to
open. Like the soft spot on a baby's skull. Like vows.
        All of the things we made ours by breaking.

WHEN THE WORLD

shows us that it's incapable
of mercy, we stay up all night
& practice how to be merciful

when it's still ninety degrees
& the constant heat is
an assault no different than living

on the sun. By fall, when hurricane season recedes,
we'll think we're alright. We'll notice
the death toll in Istanbul & Bangladesh & Baghdad

& think we're fine. The world, allowing us
thirty degree mornings, frost stiff
on the grass. We'll pull bedsheets over

the palm trees so they don't die
from the cold, as a man shoots his wife
& leaves her body in the yard, a block

away, & we'll know death isn't half
-way across the world while we're cleaning
the grout & filling up the car. Perhaps

the only mercy that matters
on this wild Gulf shore is when I ask
what you remember of snow, of digging

the car out of a ditch after we spun out
on a highway slick with black ice
& you respond with your hands

in my hair like wind that's the same
everywhere. It's what we don't say
that makes us stay. When love isn't

something done to us in the absence
of mercy, but the sun threading
the lanai after months of rain.

ii.

TRAVELING THROUGH TENNESSEE IN JANUARY

Again, I drive through dead forests
longing to flower. I think of nothing.
Not you. Not our children with their mouths
hanging half-open like shutters
over the windows, the summer
Rita followed Katrina into the Gulf
& taught us what women are capable of.
Frost on the ground, the morning after
Rita left, when it had been ninety degrees
a day before. The remains of the poor
creatures that couldn't withstand the cold,
curled on white-tipped grasses. Fields
& hills pass outside the car's windows, late
afternoon. Houses riven from each other
by land. Not water. Not here, north
of where I left you. The fields, lit from inside
as the sun slides behind hills. I try to remember
your voice. Low, like dusk. *It didn't mean anything,*
you said. But I know that you can't feel
anything & I can't feel anything
less. At the interchange of I-75 North
& I-24, I drive further into the night
from where I left you. From
where you were standing
when a voice on the radio cautioned us
against a new woman blazing
in from the east, a bloody heart
tucked between her teeth.

THE WIFE AS SCARECROW

Almost, a bridge's arches in the heather
at the nape of your neck, troubled

by sweat. Almost, my body beating
like the bird's slight body

in the country of my escape.
Almost, I climb into bed

next to you & paint myself
into the river writhing under tied arches.

Almost: light, when light never lasts.
A mountain pass. A small planet

in my throat. Almost, I know
what battles brought us here. The lake,

leaking bodies. You. A twenty-two-year-old
who couldn't swim. Your indiscretions. Almost,

I know surrender keeps me from saying,
Stay in those clothes. I can't smell her

on you. Almost, I came here as a scare
-crow. Begging the earth to hold me

upright. Begging black-feathered birds
to make a home of me.

LETTER FROM THE GULF COAST

I could be someone who twists
the truth. I knew what I was asking

when I said *Stay here with me.* The walls
waved in your image, a storm

on the horizon, growing. Hurricanes
all have their own names & we earned ours, secret

triumphs locked away in other apartments, other
cities. It wasn't having a house to tend that kept us

together. We weren't supposed to stay anywhere
long. We paint different walls the same

stark white, but they dim & darken
to a dingy beige as we stand waiting

to see what skyline comes next.
Who doesn't wake & want

to be somewhere different? Different
birds at the door. I still want your hands

on my hips. On my collarbones, arcing
toward you. A space we're meant to

dust & darken. To wake in a different city, longing
for home. Where home is the curve of our hands

on the doorknobs. Where we know ourselves
by thunder & the smell of thick

rains. By the way rain tastes as it's meant to
taste. Our mouths, upturned. Open.

ON OUR TENTH ANNIVERSARY,
MY HUSBAND & I WATCH TROPICAL STORM
ANDREA TEAR THE DOORS OFF THE LANAI

Young enough were we,
once, not to fear lightning,
pressed to our cheeks

as we knelt in the rain.
In a new version
of this story, you're still

kneeling. Featherless wings
of your fingers, flitting
under my shirt. All I can think is:

I'm a mother now. A body
without seasons. Show me
how we used to envy

rain, as it sought the storm
drains, only to resurface in a field
full of gnats. Teach me

how to hold you like water
cupped in my hands as a cure
for thirst. Let me forget, tonight,

we don't know better
hours. The earth
that bends & breaks

as we sharpen the blades
of our bodies against
shadow that swallows light.

HILLSBOROUGH COUNTY AUBADE

The night trumpets around streets & ponds. Blackbirds,
back at the door. It's midspring. The heat, already
a terrible child, bites us bare. How many times have I failed

to say *I want more in this life?* To tell you I want to wake
to a wind in which I'm seen. We have the same last name
now. Like *sin* or *burden* or *envy,* names mean nothing

when we are standing at the edge of one night, willing
ourselves into another. I bring with me thousands
of nights that flicker like votive flames around an altar.

I once let you enter & lay yourself down. I let you
be someone new. In other nights: I heard flowers bloom,
the dull sound of the suicide moon rusting in the woods.

The dead, I dragged on a leash. A man who called me
daughter. A man whose hands called my throat home. A man
who said home isn't a place I'll know. Like darkness,

I have lain still, the fog unfurling overhead. The mist burning
off the backs of the deer. We are all orphaned if we live
long enough. Time, the bell tied to our throats. Somehow,

the deer don't visit the yard now. You don't touch my throat.
Nor the night. Nor the wind in the swales. Nor the rains
that will come to stay. Nor the field I am, unable to stand.

MANNER OF DEATH

To see a hanged man—

we pity the man
& not the tree. Not the cow's-hide
belt at his throat. Not

the curse of a new season
tonguing our eyes open. Not summer
on the Gulf, slutting again. Here,

bodies stack up like hours.
The radio says a child's been
murdered by her father. A wife,

drowned. The crows seek
new casualties on street corners.
A man we know flies

to Toronto & hangs him
-self in his hotel room.
My husband crawls inside

a vacant room in his brain
that I can't enter. He mutters
on the phone about how he tried

to tell someone something
was wrong. But he's talking
about himself now & I am

the belt slipped in his belt
loops, my hands like clasps,
clenched & unforgiving.

The trees dig down deep
in wet soil outside
& I pity us all. The man & the living

thing that holds a man
as it kills him. The hour
& the hour past.

CONCEPTUAL DIAGRAM ILLUSTRATING HOW HUMANS ARE STRUCTURED AND FORMED; SEE ALSO *ADDICTION* (N) AND *STILLBIRTH* (N)

i.

With sickness the colour of rain—
when the wet season comes, we can't keep
the roof from leaking. I put duct tape over holes

in the lanai screens to keep cottonmouths
out. Wash the mold away with bleach. After
a three-year drought, we think rain is a sickness

we want, the whole world wrapped in sky.

ii.

We look for self when self
is an itinerary, not the junction
point. You numb. You savage.
I can't tell us apart
from the oaks dying in the yard.
The pretty gowns of Spanish moss
kill them faster. You want the sickness
to lay itself down inside you. I want
the child I was before I knew you. Before
the maps of ghosts & skin & cells. The saliva
tests. The doctors. Before
this sickness swam in me,
swam you, swam—

iii.

Before: we boarded the plane beside ruined wheat

  fields, a silo. Hay bales & horses. I breathed. The baby

hardened in my belly. I pictured her, furious,

  fuming. Maybe that was the moment

of her death. That laſt fight to be something

  realized. The flight took off & landed near

the Gulf. The blood was already there.

iv.

Repetition is diſtinctly human. We reach, again
& again, for our own ruin. To connect

at the damaged places we can't touch. Again,
the tiles are torn off the roof in a tropical ſtorm.

The power goes out for two days. The wind shatters
glass that isn't boarded up. Again, I get out

the ladder. I replace what is damaged. The sky
swells in the diſtance. Again, sickness takes you

from me. I tell the neighbour we're having a boy
this time. The terrible truth about childbirth

is it will never include you. The world
reimagines itself as water & rises.

THY KINGDOM COME / THY WILL BE DONE

Hallowed be the name
                    of thy children   bagged

& buried beneath snow   the woman strangled
in her bed   the child raped in a middle school

bathroom   how can you bear what you've seen
       here   o ugly snow of my childhood

tell me where my faith is buried when you go
        love   governed by seasons

I am a season   betrayed
            by sun-slits in the pavement

the sidewalks   broken   by the live oaks' lost roots
growing toward the sky   perhaps   like people

trees want more of the world
            than what they are born to

if there is a heaven   show me
        how we'll be restored   promises

like peonies   growing over gravestones   in a cemetery
      I wander   wanting

a name for my baby   that has already been claimed
surely   curses are more than myth   o lord

bless the child I carry   bless the widowed
       wind   bless the cherry blossoms   so briefly

in-bloom   bless what you've given us
bless what you take & take &

SONG FROM A DROWNING CITY (LEGATO)

Every woman begins as weather.
—Patricia Smith

Every day, the same parade
of rain. Like tongues, reckless & roiling. Every
day, you hunger the day
before. Hunger a child's vanishing
bones. Forget the revolution
of streets streaming around mail-
boxes & storm drains. Forget the sanity
of water fleeing the sky. Of dusk. Of music
sweeping thorny branches as wind
winds past lampposts & live oaks
standing sentinel. Imagine sound
didn't come from your lips. From storms
in the saints' mouths. You can suffer
anywhere. Every day you allow the clouds
this unburdening. Without
looking for god in these rituals. Every
day, forgetting there is ruin
in floods. Famine. A new feast
of flesh. Forgetting there is ruin
as you flick flies from the faces
feeding at your breasts.

PATHOLOGY

They're screaming again. Two tiny beasts
 vying for air in the living room, mouths
gaping. *It's okay,* I tell them. But

I want to turn & go. Put my coat on
 & walk out the front door to the sameness
of sidewalk squares, each quiet

seam. I want to rid myself of maternal
 breaths, the buzz in my chest
like a triple hit of adrenaline. With

each scream, I imagine a syringe unloading
 in my heart. I want to put the dirty rag
from the floor in my mouth

& stuff it down before I check to see
 what's wrong. I want to hide their tongues
inside a nesting doll & forget I ever lived

with sound. I want to say the newborn
 looks just like me, when he looks
just like a man who forced himself

inside me. The doctor says babies are
 resilient, their bones still soft
when they're first born. Sometimes,

I sit thumbing the soft spot
 on the newborn's skull, knowing his legs
can be bent at sick angles, yet one

sliver of skin is the difference
   between screaming & not screaming.
What a body can endure & what it cannot.

ALL THINGS CONSPIRE TO KEEP
SILENT ABOUT US

We won't get to choose which night ends
in fanfare. Which night ends in a hammer
to the living room walls. I want to say
I'm not afraid of loud noises after years
of being awoken in the middle of the night
sure that someone was dying. I want my hands
not to shake with violence. I've had the same dream
most of my life: I am stuck in a blizzard
with my little brother, calling & calling our dead
father for help. *Father,* as unfamiliar as flies
on my tongue, I should've known that help
only comes in the form of magazine articles
& Xanax. Sometimes, I know how to be loved. More
often, I wake to the filthy sky, food on the floor,
my son crying for someone else. I wake to a world
that has never loved anyone well. To planes & bombs
& buildings reimagined in the nostalgia of hindsight.
Winter doesn't touch me anymore. My body,
an empty cask, begs the sky to fill me
full. I am without wisdom when I am someone's
wife or mother. A woman wears a thousand names
before dying. Being called cunt by some man
who wants to look & touch like I am the display
mannequin in a department store window
is a small indignity. Everyday, I wash spit-up
from my shoulders. Cum from my stomach.
Sweat from my hair. I sleep to dream less.
I live like I am imagined.

ANNIVERSARY WITH YELLOW IRIS

In the beginning: a harp.
A haze of snow. Your hazel eyes
changing color against the back
-drop of morning before morning
was a translation for fear that weighs
down your lashes. Like hours,
the mouths we had to feed, open
& crowing. Can you still hear
the thrush thrumming the fields?
We used to wrestle with beginnings,
with night, with angels that want
no part of this world. Are there
ever enough angels? Our bodies:
churches inside churches. How
do we pray when we have no one left
to pray for? I have no patience for light.
There is never enough light.
Never enough amens that include
women & children. What can be done
about the body, about love, when either
is missing? Beginnings: the mouth,
the harp, the morning, body
counts rising like razor wire, cold
fences around us. I feel the children
who crawled out of my body
& nailed me to the sky. Back before
we argued about the train's whistle,
the stone buildings, our mothers'
bodies, the doorframes aflame,
the slam & slam. In the beginning,
I was the earthquake beneath you.

The yellow iris purifying water
in the ponds. Hours of labour
& still. Still, I remember nothing faithful
except bodies failing—my mother's, mine.
All I see are ruined trees hewn to the earth.
Is it failure when we cannot stop
reaching? Hunger-born, storm-
strewn. Savaged.

MATRIMONY AS INDEFENSIBLE HUMAN EXPERIMENT

What if I say ruin is what we wish for
when we close our eyes? What if I say
the daughter we wanted was meant

to die, even as she was suffering
& spitting & blood-stiff
as rags I used to wash the floor

when you put your forearm & fist
through the fire extinguisher's glass
face? What if I say *love*: as in missing

& mutated & flesh of our feet? What if
I say *divorce* & mean I still feel the fly
that flew into my ear canal at camp

one summer. The pain when it tried to fly
away, its wings opening & opening.
The sound of an ache no one can hear.

What if I say no. Just this once.
We have died with the birds & weather
& winter. We have died with the sky

& stars that lie as they hang themselves
against the night. What if I say *it's okay.*
Will it make me a wife? This world:

the lake, the pine trees, the prairie sky—
a proposal & an exit plan & all. What
if all that is left of me is you?

UNSIGNED LETTER TO MY STILLBORN DAUGHTER NINE YEARS LATER

After Jamaal May

Dear body of my body.
Dear fluid-breathing fauna.
Dear drowned isle in a mine
    -field of organs & feces.

I think of you often.

There was a moment in 2007, late fall, while your father worked
        overseas, that you moved, dividing yourself
from me, divorcing
my ribs, forcing my stomach up
under my full breasts.

Was it that I always wanted to be haunted?

Wanting not to be left is different.

I had a son before you & another son
        after. But the sequel is only a reminder
of what came first. Do you remember?
The kale & broccoli & hard-boiled eggs.
The punk rock anthems & lunges & jump squats.
They told me how healthy we were.
Your skinny limbs, the thumb in your mouth
articulated in the ultrasound. The eerie grey
        glow of the future I was feeding.

We were in Stockholm.
We were in Alberta.
We were in Clearwater, where the gulls
flit about the beaches & the ghost-sky hangs
        the sea.

Then, in Copenhagen, I closed my eyes, your face
pressed to my pelvis, & woke
homeless, child
-less, less & less
        a miracle.

The ugly parts of me might've been the ugly parts of you, might've
been inescapable. Like war & gunfire. As people,
we can't seem to figure out how to live
in the same spaces without killing someone
        to make more room.

My grandmother used to say: *there is a price for living
        a long life that you don't know yet, girl.*

Dear amber light, dear angel-haunt, dear
siren——,

there are days I must mother
despite the rain that chases
cockroaches inside the house. Despite
the breaths your father counts
        instead of counting heads.

I am writing to say that *human* is a fallible construct: I am
sometimes terrible, sometimes fiery, sometimes feral.

I am sometimes unable to celebrate the days
something has tried to kill me
and has failed.
Look at your brothers: their footfalls, tiny
bones. Their kindness as they tuck their hands in every crack,
as they touch us back to brave.

Here: water haunts the fields.
The dandelions, greyed & fraying.

Leaving is always delicate.

Tell me you would've given anything to stay.

Tell me, again, anyway.

TRANSVERSE ORIENTATION

This dark hour finds us fighting
over the evening's meal, the wine
bottle's wet mouth, crushed
crackers on the baby's tray.
This fight has been ours
in Stockholm, Springfield,
Copenhagen, Calgary. In the stink
of a two-story walkup, cigarette
smoke silvering the hallways, butts
littering balconies in Aalborg.
I watched you sleep, the dead rising like creeksmoke
from the cobbled streets. Now,
my son wears your face
to sleep. My breasts, heavy
with hands that paw them.
Of all of the men who have taken
from me, it is your hands
I can't forget. But these hours
have been dark longer than I am
used to. My body, a lone light
overrun by moths & mosquitoes.
You line bullets on the table
to swallow in case the head-
aches don't pass. You think
disease has set in. You're convinced
dying is this ambivalence
to light. I bathe myself in
the sink with the baby. In my skin,
I keep everything you've given me.

Each word & whisper & flicker
of your tongue. Each time you rise
in the night to cries I don't hear.
The ache of our bodies
not touching. The cities
between us. Your voice
telling our son *it's okay,*
as I pretend to sleep. Every minute
of the past that passes
in the hour farthest from
morning. It is your voice
that reaches me. That
touches me sane.

AS THE LIGHT CHANGES

Sometimes, all a woman can do is unravel
every sky to know the sky that will ſtay
when the secondhand ſtops. Pretend I'm only
one woman. I'll walk these neighbourhoods,
looking in windows for others like me. Sometimes,
I don't want to underſtand dying, while I watch my mother
lean into morning. I don't want a name for the husk
my grandmother becomes when disease enters her brain
like seawater. For spending my life leaning
into battle. In a canoe on the Hillsborough River once,
I found a Tupelo, hollowed out, & knew the pain of after-
birth. The promises our bodies make that we can't keep.
Sometimes, when I dream, I know how heaven muſt be:
somewhere & never really anywhere. The way my grandmother is
no longer a mother. The way my child grows away from me
like white smoke from a lightning ſtrike in the yard.
The closer I am to dying, I leave the ſtorm of childhood
in someone else's week. Each day, the sun growing closer
to burnout. Each day, pavement breaking in the heat.
I don't pretend to predict the future. No two deaths are alike.
Standing in the ſtreet, I liſten for the gasp of ſtorm drains
as water fills their mouths. Hard rains bending the oaks' backs.
Thunder above fields of saw grass. This grief that burns low
like smoke in the back of my throat as a hard wind rises.

NOTES

In "Self-Portrait as God with a Stillborn Inside," the italicized lines are quoted from Genesis 1:3, which refers to the first day of creation.

"Hunger [or the Last of the Daughter-Hymns]" contains Merriam Webster's dictionary definition for the word "hunger."

"The Werther Effect" epigraph is from Allison Benis White's long poem and collection *Please Bury Me in This*. The italicized line references a line in this collection.

"Fugue" references an article by Emily Van Duyne on Lit Hub titled, "Why Are We So Unwilling to Take Sylvia Plath at Her Word?"

"Why I Stay" references an article by Amy Norton on Reuters Health titled, "Couples' Risk of Breakup Higher after Pregnancy Loss."

"On Accidents & the Cold Night" concerns my paternal grandmother's experience of her three-year-old daughter's death. Mona Hrechuk was hit by a drunk driver while my grandmother Edna was at work in an industrial kitchen, cooking for the men on a construction site.

"Persistent Complex Bereavement Disorder (Complicated Grief)" references a letter from Samuel Johnson to Bennet Langton on

September 21, 1758, in which Johnson states: "the truth is, every death is violent which is the effect of accident; which is not gradually brought on by the miseries of age." From the Oxford edition of *Boswell's Life of Johnson, 1758*, edited by Jack Lynch in 1904.

"If I Had Given Her Just One Bottle, She Would Still Be Alive" takes its epigraph from the poem "Chorus" by Catherine Barnett, from her collection *Game of Boxes*. The title and subject of the poem are borrowed from several articles on Jillian Johnson and her son, Landon, titled, "If I Had Given Him Just One Bottle, He Would Still Be Alive." The premise of the articles is that Landon starved to death because breastfeeding was put to Jillian as the only acceptable way to feed her baby by the medical community.

"Let the Night Come, Monstrous, & Make Use of Us" takes its epigraph from Ben Lerner's *Angle of Yaw*. The italicized line is from Shakespeare's *Romeo and Juliet,* act 2, scene 2: "What's in a name? that which we call a rose / By any other name would smell as sweet."

"Thy Kingdom Come / Thy Will Be Done" borrows its title from the Lord's Prayer.

"Song from a Drowning City (Legato)" takes its epigraph from Patricia Smith's poem, "5 p.m., Tuesday, August 23, 2005," from the collection *Blood Dazzler*. Hurricane Katrina was the woman being referenced, but other women rocked the Gulf that year, including Rita.

"Unsigned Letter to My Stillborn Daughter Nine Years Later" is after Jamaal May's poem "Unsigned Letter to a Human in the 21st Century" from *The Big Book of Exit Strategies*. The italicized lines are from Lucille Clifton's poem, "won't you celebrate with me," from *The Collected Poems of Lucille Clifton 1965–2010*.